MW00608529

IMAGES
of America

DANDRIDGE

ON THE COVER: The Tennessee Valley Authority began construction on Douglas Dam in February 1942. The backwaters of the French Broad River would eventually flood the town of Dandridge. A town planning commission petitioned local congressmen in Washington to build a dike that would protect the town. The dike was finished in 1942, just in time to block Douglas Lake from flooding Dandridge. The dike is 900 feet long and 50 feet high. It has become a unique feature of the Dandridge landscape. (Courtesy of the Dandridge Public Library.)

IMAGES
of America

DANDRIDGE

Lisa Whillock Ellis

ARCADIA
PUBLISHING

Copyright © 2011 by Lisa Whillock Ellis
ISBN 978-1-5316-5831-1

Published by Arcadia Publishing
Charleston, South Carolina

Library of Congress Control Number: 2010933171

For all general information, please contact Arcadia Publishing:
Telephone 843-853-2070
Fax 843-853-0044
E-mail sales@arcadiapublishing.com
For customer service and orders:
Toll-Free 1-888-313-2665

Visit us on the Internet at www.arcadiapublishing.com

I would like to dedicate this book to my family, who gave me the opportunity to grow and learn in the best place on earth—Dandridge, Tennessee.

CONTENTS

ACKNOWLEDGMENTS

This book would not have been possible without the help of a group of people who love Dandridge as much as I do. They are Anne Goddard, Carolyn Ellis, John Ellis, Jim and Lu Hinchey, John Shelton, Billie Jean Chambers, Jean Gass, Jim Gass, James Saylor, Nancy Olden, and Millie Pemberton. The Dandridge Library and the Jefferson County Archives also provided invaluable resources.

INTRODUCTION

Dandridge, Tennessee, was founded in 1783, which was 13 years before the establishment of the State of Tennessee. It began as a small frontier settlement along the banks of the French Broad River in the short lived State of Franklin. Dandridge is the second oldest town in Tennessee. Jonesborough, founded in 1779, is the oldest town in the state. In 1793, Dandridge became the county seat for the newly formed Jefferson County. Jefferson County was named for the then secretary of state, Thomas Jefferson. The town itself was named for First Lady Martha Dandridge Custis Washington and remains the only town in the United States that bears her name.

Education has always been a priority in Dandridge. Maury Academy was established in 1806. It was the center of education for the Dandridge area. In 1950, Maury High School was built and the academy was used for lower grades. Early businesses were mostly taverns and inns, built to accommodate travelers. Eventually town commerce expanded to dry goods, drugstores, grocery, and hardware. There are a variety of architectural styles in Dandridge, which include the following: Federal, Greek, Victorian, and the 20th-century arts and crafts period. The courthouse is an excellent example of the Greek Revival style. It houses a museum that showcases many relics that chronicle the history of the town.

In December 1863, the Confederates in Dandridge intercepted Union general Ambrose Burnside's troops. The Confederates, led by Gen. James Longstreet, forced the Union army northwest to New Market. This area was affected by the Civil War in other ways. Many families in East Tennessee supported the Union. This caused families to split and neighbors to rally against each other. Many notable people made their homes in Dandridge. Davy Crockett married his first wife, Polly Finley, near Dandridge, and the courthouse still has his marriage bond in its archives. The courthouse also contains an earlier marriage bond from 1805 between Crockett and Margaret Elder. This marriage never took place. Samuel McSpadden built his home in 1804 on the banks of the French Broad River. He operated a gunpowder mill and supplied Andrew Jackson's forces in New Orleans during the War of 1812. Writer Bert Vincent is a household name among East Tennesseans. From 1929 until his death in 1969, he wrote a column called Strolling for the *Knoxville News-Sentinel*. Vincent's stories were folk stories and Appalachian yarns. Frank Quarles served as Jefferson County sheriff, U.S. Marshal, state representative, and state senator. In August 26, 1956, Clinton High School made history by becoming the first public high school in the South to desegregate. Marshal Quarles was sent to Clinton to keep peace among the growing crowd of protesters.

The federal government established the Tennessee Valley Authority (TVA) in 1933. Its purpose was to provide flood control, navigation, electrical generation, and economic development in the Tennessee Valley. Douglas Dam was built in 1942, just southwest of Dandridge. Due to its proximity to the French Broad River, Dandridge would be several feet below the high water mark of the lake. A planning commission contacted local congressmen for help in saving the small East Tennessee town. A dike was constructed and it continues to be an interesting feature of Dandridge. A small glass square in the courthouse's second step shows where the high water mark would have been without the dike. Dandridge is on the National Register of Historical Places and hosts several festivals each year. Douglas Lake makes the town a popular spot for recreation. Even after 228 years, Dandridge continues to be a very special town to many people. Its charm and tradition will hopefully live on for another 228 years.

One

EARLY DAYS

The first inhabitants of the area of Dandridge were Native Americans. They lived in communities along the French Broad River. Over 200 years later, Scotch-Irish settlers crossed the Appalachian Mountains to establish communities along the same river. Dandridge was settled in 1783, which was one year before the formation of the State of Franklin. It was incorporated in 1793, which was three years before the establishment of the State of Tennessee. Dandridge thrived through the following years and survived a Civil War battle in the winter of 1864.

In the 1930s, the federal government provided funding under the Works Progress Administration (WPA) for archeological digs in places such as the Tennessee Valley. Shown here is a Native American burial mound at the Zimmerman's Island site. Zimmerman's Island was located just upstream from the Douglas Dam and was excavated in 1942. (Courtesy of Frank H. McClung Museum, the University of Tennessee, Knoxville.)

Here is a crew at the Fain's Island dig. The WPA program provided jobs for the unemployed during the Depression. Fain's Island is located just downstream from Dandridge and just upstream from Shadden Creek. (Courtesy of Frank H. McClung Museum, the University of Tennessee, Knoxville.)

This 1935 photograph shows post molds of a structure at Fain's Island. The posts would have been from some type of Cahokia structure on the island. Notice the cornfield in the background. The Cahokias were a population of Late Mississippian period Native Americans, who inhabited the Tennessee Valley from 1400 to about 1539. (Courtesy of Frank H. McClung Museum, the University of Tennessee, Knoxville.)

Here the dig crew poses in a hardpan pit on Fain's Island. Hardpan refers to the dense, compacted layer of soil under the uppermost layer of topsoil. (Courtesy of Frank H. McClung Museum, the University of Tennessee, Knoxville.)

These are the hardpan pits of a second slice. This photograph shows excavated burial sites on Fain's Island during the 1935 dig. (Courtesy of Frank H. McClung Museum, the University of Tennessee, Knoxville.)

This fire pit was excavated in 1935 on Fain's Island. It was made of hard baked red clay and sand. (Courtesy of Frank H. McClung Museum, the University of Tennessee, Knoxville.)

This is a typical campsite of a 1930s archeological crew. The cook is standing in the middle of the group holding a large knife and honing steel. All the men are wearing sturdy, lace-up boots. The man on the far left is smoking a pipe. This photograph was taken in 1935. (Courtesy of Frank H. McClung Museum, the University of Tennessee, Knoxville.)

m. Washington

The city of Dandridge was named for Martha Dandridge Custis Washington. She was born in Virginia in 1731. Her father, John Dandridge, immigrated to Virginia from England around 1716. She married Daniel Parke Custis in 1750. Custis died in 1757. She then married Col. George Washington in 1759 and became the nation's first First Lady of the United States in 1789. She died at Mount Vernon May 22, 1802. (Courtesy of the Library of Congress.)

This marker commemorates the original founders of Dandridge. These men fought in the Revolutionary War and are buried in the Revolutionary Cemetery in the center of town, near the original site of Rev. Robert Henderson's Lower Meeting House. James McCuistion, another of the founders, is also buried here. The Martha Dandridge Garden Club commissioned the marker in the 1920s. (Courtesy of Lisa Ellis.)

This spring was on the property of the Lower Meeting House. It was a good source of drinking water and was one of the major factors in choosing the site for the new town. The Hynds House can be seen in the background. (Courtesy of the Jefferson County Archives.)

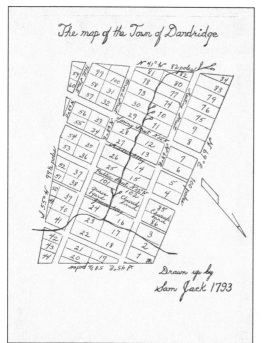

The map of the Town of Dandridge

Drawn up by
Sam Jack 1793

In the spring of 1793, a committee was appointed by the court of the newly formed Jefferson County to plan a new town that would become the county seat. Francis Dean donated 50 acres of land on the French Broad River. Surveyor Samuel Jack was paid $10 to draw up the plat for the town. The original has been preserved in the courthouse. (Courtesy of the Jefferson County Archives.)

The second county court, which established Jefferson County, was held at this house in 1793. Since the end of the Civil War, this house has been known as the Billy Blue House. Billy Blue was a freed slave. His parents were given the house by the Inman family after the Civil War. It was located on lot 26, just west of the courthouse. (Courtesy of the Dandridge Public Library.)

Davy Crockett, frontiersman and hero of the Alamo, lived for a time in Jefferson County. In 1806, he obtained a marriage bond to Polly Finley at the Jefferson County Courthouse in Dandridge. This was not the first marriage bond that Davy applied for. The year before, he applied for another bond to marry Margaret Elder. Margaret married someone else and her marriage to Davy never took place. Davy and Polly lived in Jefferson County until 1812. The first two of their three children, John and William, were born here. Both marriage bonds are still kept in the Jefferson County Courthouse. (Courtesy of the Library of Congress.)

Know all men by these presents that we Davie Crockett and Thomas Doggett are held and firmly bound unto John Sevier Governor and his successors in office in the sum of Twelve hundred fifty Dollars to be void on condition there be no cause to obstruct the marriage of the said Davie Crockett with Polly Findley. Witness our hands and seals this 12th day of August 1806

Test
J. Hamilton

Davie Crockett

Thos x Doggett
his
mark

This is a copy of the marriage bond between Davy Crockett and Polly Finley. They were married for nine years. Polly died in 1815. In 1816, he married Elizabeth Patton, a widow with two children. They moved to Western Tennessee in 1817. (Courtesy of the Jefferson County Archives.)

This bench is one of several located in the Revolutionary Cemetery. The garden club placed the benches there in the 1920s. Shepard's Inn can be seen in the background. The brick section served as the kitchen. (Courtesy of Lisa Ellis.)

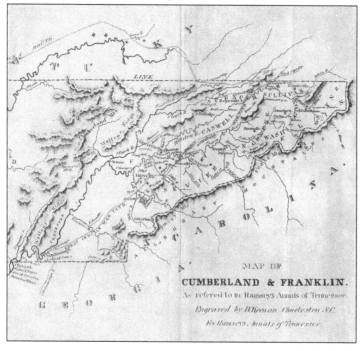

This map shows the state of Franklin. Dandridge is shown in Caswell County on the Great Indian War Path. Franklin was created in 1784 from land west of the Appalachians that was part of North Carolina. In 1790, it became part of North Carolina once again. The state of Tennessee was formed in 1796 from the original state of Franklin. (Courtesy of the East Tennessee Historical Society.)

Ellen Hynds Vincent is seen posing in the courthouse with the original marriage bond of Davy Crockett and Polly Finley. She was a descendant of Judge Robert Henry Hynds and was the wife of writer Bert Vincent. Ellen lived in the Hynds House until her death in 1979.

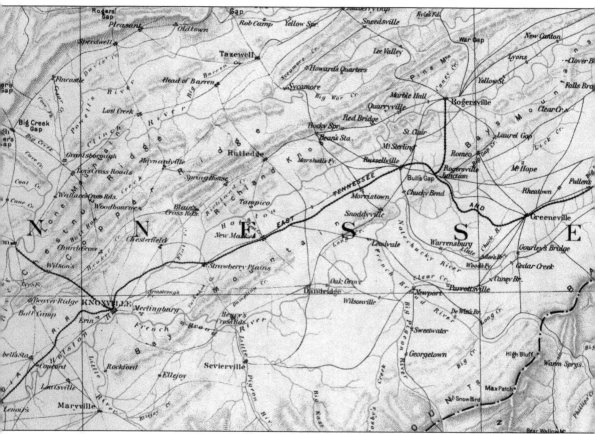

This Civil War map shows many East Tennessee cities and towns during the Civil War. Dandridge was the site of a minor Civil War battle during the winter of 1863–1864. (Courtesy of the East Tennessee Historical Society.)

Confederate general James Longstreet served under Gen. Robert E. Lee, who referred to him as the "old war horse." He was the commanding general during the Knoxville Campaign in the fall of 1863. Union forces under Gen. Ambrose Burnside held the city. Longstreet commanded the Confederate forces during the Battle of Dandridge. (Courtesy of the Abraham Lincoln Library and Museum of Lincoln Memorial University, Harrogate, Tennessee.)

Union general John Park commanded the Union forces during the Battle of Dandridge. In January 1864, Parke met with his commanders in the Hynds House. Because of the weather and word that Longstreet had reinforcements, Parke and his men decided to withdraw to Strawberry Plains. (Courtesy of the Abraham Lincoln Library and Museum of Lincoln Memorial University, Harrogate, Tennessee.)

21

This unidentified photograph was taken in front of the courthouse in the late 19th century. It is possible that this could have been a reunion of Civil War veterans. They were common throughout the United States until the 1930s. (Courtesy of the Jefferson County Archives.)

Two

CHURCHES

Dandridge was founded on the grounds of Henderson's Lower Meeting House. This church formed the roots of Hopewell Presbyterian. Over the years, other congregations formed and were supported by a community deeply rooted in the Christian Faith. Issues like slavery and the Civil War sometimes separated congregations. Still they reunited to form an even stronger bond. Many of the old congregations still survive today, providing Dandridge with a strong sense of community and support.

First Presbyterian Church, Dandridge, Tenn.

Presbyterian Church-Dandridge, Tenn.

Here is a postcard view of Hopewell Presbyterian Church. Hopewell was never the First Presbyterian Church. Organized in 1785, it started as Henderson's Lower Meeting House. The church was moved to its present location in 1842. The congregation split during the Civil War but recovered. The present brick sanctuary replaced the white frame one after it burned in 1868. Hopewell is the oldest congregation in Dandridge. (Courtesy of Anne Goddard Jones.)

This photograph of Hopewell Presbyterian was taken in 1938. The building had not changed much in 66 years. (Courtesy of Anne Goddard Jones.)

Roy Farrar Sr. is standing at the front door of the Presbyterian church in the 1950s. Roy was the first licensed embalmer in Jefferson County. (Courtesy of Jack Farrar.)

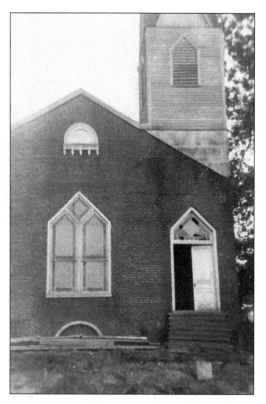

The Methodist Church split in 1845 over the issue of slavery. The Methodist Episcopal Church South continued to meet in this building until 1942. The Tennessee Valley Authority razed the church for construction of the dike. (Courtesy of Jean Gass.)

Here members of the Gass family stand on the front steps of the Methodist Episcopal Church South around 1940. Included in the photograph are, from left to right, (first row) Margaret Gass and unidentified; (second row) Hattie and Frank Gass; (third row) Cora and Raymond Gass; (fourth row) two unidentified and Merle "Zoom" Gass. (Courtesy of Jean Gass.)

This early photograph shows the First United Methodist Church. The church was established in 1805 and split in 1845 over the issue of slavery. The clapboard sanctuary was built around 1900, and brick replaced the clapboard in 1942. (Courtesy of the Jefferson County Archives.)

The United Methodist Church continued to meet in this sanctuary until 1983. A new sanctuary was built on adjacent property, which had been owned by the Raymond Gass family. (Courtesy of the Jefferson County Archives.)

This early photograph shows the Dandridge Baptist Church. This building was located on Church Street and was in use from 1845 until it was destroyed by fire in 1913. (Courtesy of the Tennessee State Library and Archives.)

The third Baptist Church Building was built on the site of the one destroyed by fire. It was completed in 1914. In 1958, the name was changed to the First Baptist Church of Dandridge. In 1983, a new sanctuary was built on Highway 92. The stained-glass windows from the old church were used in construction of the new building. (Courtesy of the Tennessee State Library and Archives.)

Bethel Presbyterian Church broke off from Hopewell Presbyterian Church after the Civil War. The African American Presbyterian congregation worshiped in two places until 1880 when Thomas Fain laid the foundation for the current building. The original building is still in use by the congregation. (Courtesy of the Jefferson County Archives.)

Kate Slover Rimmer and her son Gene pose in front of Bethel Presbyterian Church. The building on the far right was the Christ Temple African Methodist Episcopal Zion Church. It was torn down in 1912, when the property was bought by the city for construction of a new high school. A new church building was constructed on the east side of town. (Courtesy of the Dandridge Public Library.)

Three

SCHOOLS

The early settlers understood the importance of education. Early on, they formed a school in a log cabin near the center of town. A few years later, state funding provided for a wood frame building. In 1819, a brick building was erected. Whether it was the academy, the Female Academy, the high school, or the middle school, Maury is a name familiar to everyone who attended school in Dandridge. The education provided in Dandridge has given the world doctors, lawyers, teachers, and even a university president.

This postcard image shows the old Masonic Hall. The building was located where the library is today. The school in Dandridge was coeducational until 1840, when the Masons provided space for the Dandridge Female Academy in their building. The school continued until the late 1930s. The building was torn down in the early 1940s because of TVA construction. (Courtesy of Anne Goddard Jones.)

This is a 1910 postcard view of Maury Academy. In 1884, the upper grades from the Female Academy returned to Maury Academy and the lower grades remained at the Female Academy. This building replaced the old academy that was built in 1819. (Courtesy of Anne Goddard Jones.)

This photograph of Maury Academy was taken in the 1940s. The WPA built the wall in the foreground in the 1930s. (Courtesy of the Dandridge Public Library.)

Faculty members of Maury Academy pose in front of the school in 1920. Principal Elmer Goddard is on the far left. (Courtesy of the Dandridge Public Library.)

The children in this photograph are dressed for a pageant. They are standing beside Hopewell Church in the early 1900s. (Courtesy of the Dandridge Public Library.)

This high school was built in 1927. Barber and McMurray, well known architects from Knoxville, designed the building. The old academy building was used as an elementary school. (Courtesy of Anne Goddard Jones.)

This is the Maury High School Class of 1935. There were 32 graduates that year. (Courtesy of Carolyn Ellis.)

Students of Maury Academy performed a Tom Thumb wedding in 1937. Those identified are (first row) Ema Rae Northern, Pat Northern, Richard Potts, Mary Jean Reese, Mildred Kane, and Margaret Gass; (second row) Robert and Richard Baker, Katherine and Ruth Blackburn, Jackie Henry, Joanna Petree, Doris Abernathy, and Kyle Swann; (third row) John Thompson, Anne Owens, John Chesteen, Bobbie Griffie, Stephen Kane, Barbara Vineyard, Peggy Chesteen, Merle Lee Gass, and Mildred Lethco. (Courtesy of Millie Pemberton.)

Wylie Quarles wears a Maury letter sweater in 1937. He is standing in front of the Maury High School. (Courtesy of Carolyn Ellis.)

These coeds joke around in front of Maury High School in 1947. From left to right are Doris Fain, Elsie Jane Rimmer, Carolyn Quarles, Emma Rae Northern, and Essie Mae Roberts. (Courtesy of Carolyn Ellis.)

This is the 1948–1949 Maury girls basketball team. From left to right, those identified are Carolyn Quarles, second; Rae Northern, third; Stella Dockery, fifth; Millie Kane, seventh; Billie Rimmer, eighth; Ester Ann Moore, ninth; Essie Roberts, tenth; and Bobbie Carmichael, twelfth. Chan Huskey was the coach and Patsy Northern was manager. (Courtesy of Carolyn Ellis.)

Here is the 1951 Maury High School basketball Team. From front to back, those identified are Bobbie Carmichael, first; Essie Roberts, sixth; Carolyn Clevenger, eighth; Rae Northern, ninth; and Carolyn Quarles, twelfth. (Courtesy of Millie Pemberton.)

African American children attended Riverview School before desegregation. The school was located on a bluff near the French Broad River. Grades one through four were located in the room on the right side of the building. Grades five through eight were on the left side. After the desegregation act closed the school in 1965, the building became the county Agricultural Extension Office. (Courtesy of Dandridge Public Library.)

These two ladies pose at the front of Riverview School in the 1950s. Addie Bragg is standing on the porch. (Courtesy of Dandridge Public Library.)

This class photograph was taken around 1940. Those pictured are, from left to right, (first row) Arvil Lee Webb, Mary Taylor, Ottis Dean Bragg, Nancy Shefield, and Annie May Webb; (second row) George Bragg, Mary Julia Fain, Dave Taylor, and Bob Bragg; (third row) Robert Napolian Shefield, Alfred Webb, James Taylor, Chester Bragg, Clarence James, and Dale Branner; (fourth row) Clarence Ballenger and Raymond Bragg. (Courtesy of Dandridge Public Library.)

These children play a game of baseball at Riverview School in the 1940s. Oscar Shefield in on the far left. (Courtesy of Dandridge Public Library.)

Louise Snodderly served as the librarian at Maury High School. This photograph was taken in 1954. The school opened its doors on January 2, 1951. It became Maury Middle School in the fall of 1975, after Jefferson County High School was built. (Courtesy of Dandridge Public Library.)

John Stokely Jr. was the principal at Maury High School in the 1950s. (Courtesy of *Maury Hi-Life*.)

Superintendent Y. J. McAndrew; his wife, Barbra; and former superintendent Elmer Goddard (third from right) attend the Parent-Teacher Association (PTA) meeting in the Dandridge Elementary Cafeteria. Elmer Goddard served as superintendant from 1922 to 1930. Y. J. McAndrew served from 1956 until 1972. (Courtesy of Dandridge Public Library.)

Ruth Goddard (third from left) looks on as a Mr. and Mrs. Carpenter prepare to speak at a PTA meeting in the mid-1950s. (Courtesy of Dandridge Public Library.)

This snowy scene is looking east toward town. Bethel Church is to the left, and Maury academy is just past it. Downtown Dandridge is to the right. The Routh-Creswell House is just to the left of the tree. (Courtesy of Dandridge Public Library.)

Seen here with faculty sponsors Jack Pemberton (first row, left), Martha Lou Coile (second row, left), and Virginia Hodges (second row, second from left) are the junior class officers for 1956. They are, from left to right, (first row) vice president Ernest Bishop; secretary Tom White; and president Ronnie French; (second row) reporter Ruth Reneau and treasurer Norma French. (Courtesy of *Maury Hi-Life*.)

Harriet Blackburn taught civics, history, and English. She continued to teach at Maury High School into the 1970s. (Courtesy of *Maury Hi-Life*.)

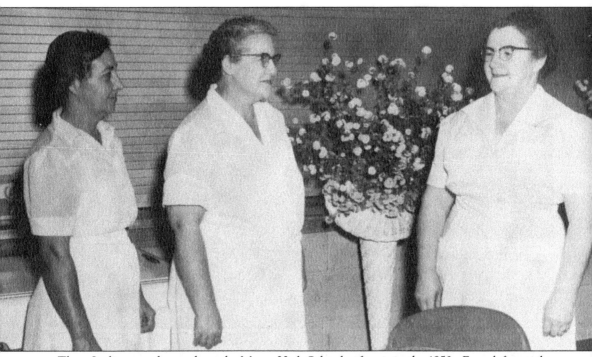

These Ladies served as cooks at the Maury High School cafeteria in the 1950s. From left to right are Annie Potter, Kathleen White, and Lizzie Miller. (Courtesy of *Maury Hi-Life*.)

Jack Pemberton taught health and physical education, in addition to serving as an assistant football and basketball coach. (Courtesy of *Maury Hi-Life*.)

W. F. Bales Jr. was the head football coach for the Maury Hornets. He also taught economics and physical education. (Courtesy of *Maury Hi-Life*.)

Four

COMMERCE

Some of the first businesses in Dandridge were taverns. These taverns served the stagecoach traffic from Knoxville to Abingdon, Virginia. The French Broad River provided a means of transporting goods to town. Dandridge was self-supporting. There were inns, dry goods stores, tanneries, and livery stables. Later businesses included car dealerships, gas stations, drugstores, and even a movie theater. Business continues to thrive. Today there are no taverns in Dandridge, but people can still have a great milk shake at the local drugstore.

This was the original site of Lovisca Seahorn's tavern. She served food and stabled horses here beginning in 1816. Later Shadrach Inman and William Harris operated a general store here. In the 1890s, the Gass family bought the property and ran a general store in this building for over 100 years. (Courtesy of Anne Goddard Jones.)

A Steamboat carried passengers and goods to and from Knoxville on the French Broad River. The whistle could be heard from far down the river, even before the boat was in sight. (Courtesy of Dandridge Public Library.)

The Vance Building was built in the early 1820s in the Federal style. Visible on the outside are signs advertising furniture and ladies' hats. The post office was located here, as well as a funeral parlor. This building also housed the switchboard. A sign on the far left side of the building is for the telephone's office. Pet Swann operated the switchboard. (Courtesy of the Jefferson County Archives.)

The Colvin house was located on the west side of the Vance Building on Main Street. It was used as a boardinghouse for the students at Maury Academy. The east side was for male students, and the female students were housed on the south side. It was torn down around 1942, and Jefferson County Motors was built on the site. (Courtesy of the Jefferson County Archives.)

This photograph shows Bud Miller (left) and Bob Swann with the first bottle of whisky made at the legal distillery located south of the river. Bill Swann owned the distillery. Another legal distillery was about 7 miles west of Dandridge in the Piedmont community. William Whillock owned it. (Courtesy of the Tennessee State Library and Archives.)

This view is looking east at the intersection of Gay Street and Main Street. The Gass dry goods store is on the right. The brick building on the left is part of the block that burned in a 1910 fire. The block was rebuilt and still stands today. (Courtesy of Anne Goddard Jones.)

Shepard's Inn was originally the site of Mitchell Tavern. Shadrach Inman built a log cabin on the site. Eventually a Victorian structure was built around the cabin. It was sold to James Mitchell, who operated a tavern there. (Courtesy of Anne Goddard Jones.)

The Licklyter Stable was located on the east side of Gay Street, next to the Hynds House. It was one of several in town. (Courtesy of the Dandridge Public Library.)

In the early 1900s, the Episcopal Methodist Church South can be seen in the background, looking east down Main Street. The Rogers-Miller house is on the left, and Roper Mansion is further done the street on the same side. The courthouse cupola is seen through the trees. (Courtesy of Jean Gass.)

This is the John M. Hill Feed and Livery Stable around 1910. Shown are, from left to right, John Martin Hill, Captain Holtsinger, Ralph Rainwater, and Dick Bradford. (Courtesy of the Tennessee State Library and Archives.)

Here are the clerks at the Gass dry goods store. The milliner is sitting in a chair decorating a hat. The store sold domestic goods and women's, men's and children's clothes and shoes. (Courtesy of the Jefferson County Archives.)

This early-20th-century photograph shows Gay Street, looking south. Thomas Tavern is barely visible on the far left. The Hynds House is on the middle left side. The Central Hotel and Rainwater Livery are on the right. The Female Academy is shown on the hill beyond the courthouse, with the Frank Gass house on the far left. (Courtesy of Jean Gass.)

This advertisement is the for Gass dry goods store. It was published in the *Newport Plain Talk* on March 31, 1915. (Courtesy of the *Newport Plain Talk*.)

This is Shepard's Inn around 1900. Notice how rugged Main Street looks and the fence around the Revolutionary Cemetery. This photograph was made before an addition connected the main inn with the brick kitchen at the back. (Courtesy of Nancy Olden.)

This view is looking north on Gay Street around 1914. The Gass dry goods building is located in the lower right corner. The Vance Building and courthouse are on the left side. The row of brick buildings on the right now houses a real estate office and Tinsley-Bible Drugstore. The Hynds House and Thomas Tavern are visible beyond the brick storefronts. Note the automobile parked on Gay Street. (Courtesy of the Jefferson County Archives.)

This photograph shows "Granny" Kate Peck on the porch of the Shepard's Inn in the early 1900s. She was the cook there for many years. (Courtesy of Nancy Olden.)

B3607   Main Street. Dandridge. Tenn.

Even though the title says Main Street, this postcard actually shows the storefronts on Gay Street. The second building from the left housed the Tinsley Drugstore. Right next to it is a dry goods and grocery store. The stores eventually combined to form Tinsley-Bible Drugstore. (Courtesy of Nancy Olden.)

B2246 Court House, Dandridge, Tenn.

Here is an early 20th-century view of the courthouse. The Vance Building is located on the left. Hubert Mills, an employee of the telephone company, is the man on the telephone line. Telephone service first came to Dandridge in 1903. (Courtesy of the Dandridge Public Library.)

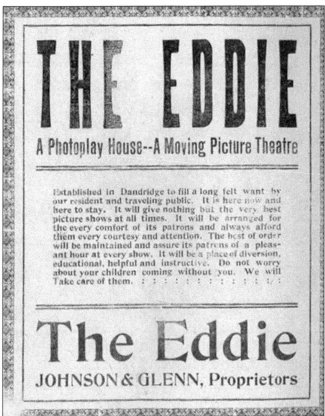

The Eddie was a "moving picture theater" that was located on Highway 70, near Hopewell Street. This advertisement is from 1915. (Courtesy of the *Newport Plain Talk*.)

Shepard's Inn was a popular destination for travelers and those looking for a good meal. Notice the American Automobile Association and Bell Telephone signs hanging in front. Also a small addition has been added to the back. (Courtesy of Anne Goddard Jones.)

This photograph of an unidentified office showcases a new technology—electricity. Notice the electric lights and wires that are strung around the room. Also there are gas light fixtures suspended from the ceiling. The photograph was probably taken around 1915, just after electricity became available in Dandridge. (Courtesy of the Jefferson County Archives.)

This is a 1915 advertisement for the Holtsinger and Cox "Buick Garage." This was one of two car dealerships in town. (Courtesy of the *Newport Plain Talk*.)

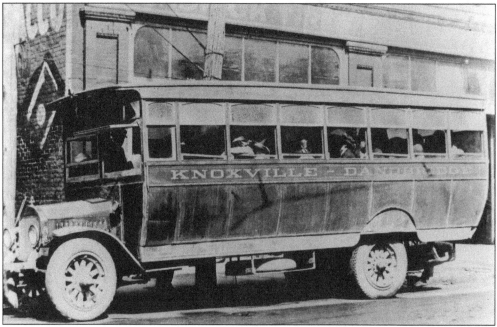

Even though the railroad was built across the northern section of Jefferson County through Jefferson City, many workers commuted daily from Dandridge to Knoxville by bus. The bus that is shown dates from the 1920s. This service continued until the 1960s. (Courtesy of Dandridge Public Library.)

Gass and Owens were agents for the Overland-Ford dealership. Art Kane eventually owned the local Ford dealership. The Overland was produced until 1926. (Courtesy of Dandridge Public Library.)

G. W. Rimmer, pictured on the left, is shown at his store, G. W. Rimmer Fine Groceries. This photograph was taken in 1920. (Courtesy of the Tennessee State Library and Archives.)

This view is looking west along Highway 25/70 in 1938. This was the main route between Knoxville and Asheville, North Carolina, until Interstate 40 was completed through Jefferson County in 1975. The Gulf Station, on the left, no longer sells gas but is a mechanic shop. Thomas Tavern is just beyond. The frame structure on the right is no longer there. (Courtesy of the National Archives, Atlanta.)

Arthur F. Kane founded the Jefferson County Motor Company in 1929. The original building was next to Hickman Tavern. When the dike was built, Arthur moved his dealership to the lot across the street from the courthouse, which was where the Colvin house had been. (Courtesy of Millie Pemberton.)

The Strange Grocery Store was one of many businesses located in the Vance Building since it was built in 1823. Pictured are Donald and Kathleen Strange Brimer who ran the store. Kathleen's father owned it. This photograph is from 1939. (Courtesy of Dandridge Public Library.)

This photograph was taken around 1950. The White Store was a popular chain of grocery stores in East Tennessee. It had three locations in Dandridge. The first location was here on Gay Street. Allen Hankins was the manager and well known to all in Dandridge. Later this was the location of the Five and Dime Store, which was also known as the dime store. This store was a favorite of the local children and was owned by Brad Evans. (Courtesy of the Jefferson County Archives.)

This was the new home of Jefferson County Motors. This building was opened in 1945 after the first building was torn down for the construction of the dike. (Courtesy of Millie Pemberton.)

The Dandridge Service Station was located on Highway 25/70. The manager was R. P. Potts. (Courtesy of the Jefferson County Archives.)

This is a view of the Vance Building in the 1970s. Notice that the door in front has been converted to a window and the cellar windows have been covered. Also the window on the left side has been enlarged. The building has since been restored. (Courtesy of the Jefferson County Archives.)

Swann's Farm Market offered a variety of produce. It was located on Highway 70, near Dandridge. This photograph was taken in August 1950. (Courtesy of the Tennessee State Library and Archives.)

In the 1920s, the local grocery store held a drawing every Saturday from the courthouse steps. Names were written on receipts during the week. The winner of the drawing would receive $5 in cash. (Courtesy of Anne Goddard Jones.)

This hearse belonged to Farrar Funeral Home. This photograph was made in the mid-1950s.
(Courtesy of Jack Farrar.)

Farrar Funeral Home opened in 1945 in Dandridge. The funeral home was first located in the Chesteen house on Hopewell Street. Later it was moved to its present location on Meeting Street. (Courtesy of Jack Farrar.)

This postcard shows a couple at the Swann Farms Boat Dock and Cabins on Douglas Lake. It was located near Swann's Farm Market. (Courtesy of Anne Goddard Jones.)

This aerial view is of Galloway's Landing. The marina included "modern cabins" and "good fishing." It was located just across the lake from Dandridge on the present site of the Point restaurant. (Courtesy of Anne Goddard Jones.)

Downtown Dandridge in the 1970s looked much as it did at the beginning of the 20th century. The livery stables and the Female Academy are gone, but landmarks like the courthouse and the Hynds House are still there. (Courtesy of Jean Gass.)

Here is the Gass dry goods store as it appeared in the 1970s. The store was closed in 1983 after the death of Raymond Gass. (Courtesy of Jean Gass.)

Five

ARCHITECTURE

The earliest dwellings in Dandridge were made of logs. Many of these still exist, protected under the wood framework of beautiful Victorian homes. The Federal style is seen in city hall, which was once Hickman Tavern. The courthouse is a classic example of the Greek Revival style. Dandridge is fortunate that many of these buildings have been preserved. Styles such as the bungalow and the mid-century modern add to the evolution of architecture that started with the first log cabin back in 1783.

The Routh-Creswell House was originally a log home. Modern siding covers the logs. Built in 1800, it was the site of White's Tannery. (Courtesy of the Jefferson County Archives.)

Mitchell Tavern began as a two-story log structure. The original logs can be found under the weather boarding. James Mitchell bought it in 1852. He operated a tavern there until 1892. The Shepard family operated it as an inn for several years. (Courtesy of the Jefferson County Archives.)

The Jerome Gass–Thula Swann House was built in 1820. The Victorian brick has four pilasters across the front. The ornate front porch is typical of the Victorian style. (Courtesy of the Jefferson County Archives.)

The Fain family built Hickman Tavern in the early 1820s. It served travelers on the route from Knoxville to Abingdon, Virginia. Francis Hickman later bought the tavern. It has served as a community center and now is the town hall. (Courtesy of Anne Goddard Jones.)

The 1882 Building is another excellent example of Victoria architecture in Dandridge. Over the past 128 years, it has been the site of a doctor's office, the post office, a restaurant, and a flower shop. (Courtesy of the Tennessee State Library and Archives.)

John Roper built Roper Mansion in 1821. It is a large, Federal-style house and boasts a brick cornice with sidelights and transom around the front door. Roper, a prominent Dandridge businessman, was president of the Bank of Dandridge. This was the first bank in Jefferson County. (Courtesy of the Jefferson County Archives.)

The Holtsinger house, one of the earliest frame houses, was originally a log house. G. W. Holtsinger, who was clerk and master for the Jefferson County Court, owned it. (Courtesy of the Tennessee State Library and Archives.)

The Hickman Brothers built the courthouse in 1845. The bricks were locally made. It is in the Greek Revival style, which was popular from the early to mid-19th century. It replaced an earlier structure. The courthouse is the one of the oldest courthouses in the country that is still in use. There is a museum on the first floor that contains interesting objects that chronicle the history of Jefferson County. (Courtesy of Anne Goddard Jones.)

Samuel McCuistion built the McCuistion house in 1847. He was the clerk of the register and the circuit court clerk of Jefferson County. It is said that McCuistion's father bought Davy Crockett's gun so Crockett could afford to marry Polly Finley in 1806. (Courtesy of the Jefferson County Archives.)

James Seabolt built the Seabolt-Harris in 1848. It has an impressive two-story portico with a classic pediment. During the Civil War it was used as a hospital. Eventually the Harris family acquired it and its member lived there for many years. An addition was added to the back of the house in 1926. (Courtesy of the Jefferson County Archives.)

Dr. Samuel Fain built this house in 1843. It is of the Georgian style, and the bricks were made on the farm. The porch includes four Ionic-style columns. (Courtesy of the Jefferson County Archives.)

This photograph shows Ann Swann Shuler standing next to a large boxwood at Squirewood in the 1920s. Squirewood is the Georgian-style house built in 1860 by federal judge James Preston Swann. (Courtesy of the Dandridge Public Library.)

The Thomas Tavern dates from the early 1800s. James Mitchell built a log tavern on the land that he bought from the Presbyterian Church. Later Mitchell would buy a two-story house from Sharach Inman that would become known as the Mitchell house. (Courtesy of the Jefferson County Archives.)

This is the north parlor of the Hynds House in the 1950s. It was then the home of writer Bert Vincent and his wife, Ellen Hynds Vincent. (Courtesy of the University Archives, Carnegie-Vincent Library of Lincoln Memorial University, Harrogate, Tennessee.)

The home of Dr. James Nathaniel Lyle, a Civil War doctor, was also known as the "Button Lyle house" or the "house of seven porches." The home was used as a hospital. Patients could relax on one of the porches during recovery. It was located above the French Broad River on what is now Lake Shore Drive. The house was eventually torn down to make room for a modern home. (Courtesy of the Dandridge Public Library.)

This photograph was taken in the early 19th century from the roof of a house on Main Street. The home on the left is the Rogers-Miller house. On the left is a frame house that was owned by Elizabeth Hill Best. The courthouse can be seen on the far right. On the street, notice the horse and buggy that were blurred by the slow camera shutter. (Courtesy of the Dandridge Public Library.)

The Lyle house was an ornate Victorian home. This photograph was made in the early 1900s. (Courtesy of the Dandridge Public Library.)

Dr. Sam Sullenberger bought the Lyle house and founded the Sullenberger Hospital. It was closed after he died in 1960. The house burned down in the mid-1960s. (Courtesy of Millie Pemberton.)

Frank L. and Hattie Fox Gass's home was built around 1900. It was located on the spot where the Jefferson County Bank Building was built in the 1950s. The house is also seen in the background of the photograph on the cover. (Courtesy of Jean Gass.)

This was the home of Raymond and Cora Gass and their two children, Merle and Margaret. The United Methodist Church acquired the property in 1983. This is the current location of the Methodist Sanctuary. (Courtesy of Jean Gass.)

The Chesteen house was built in 1900. It was the original location of Farrar Funeral Home. (Courtesy of the Jefferson County Archives.)

Sam Bettis built the hexagon house in 1905. It is an unusual style for a town that features several classic Victorian and Federal styles. Each of the five-sided rooms has one short wall. The chimney is in the center of the house. (Courtesy of the Dandridge Public Library.)

Here is an early Dandridge street scene from around 1910. The road is not paved and the sidewalks are plank. About nine years later, telephone poles would be erected. Telephone service arrived in Dandridge on February 14, 1901. (Courtesy of Millie Pemberton.)

This early 1940s view of downtown was taken from the vantage point in front of Maury Academy. In the distance is Douglas Lake. The Frank Gass house can be seen just beyond the roofline of the courthouse. The Colvin house stands across the street and is to the right of the courthouse. (Courtesy of the Dandridge Public Library.)

This was the home of Arthur and Lena Kane. The photograph was made in the summer of 1946. An interesting feature is the millstone that is embedded in the front walk. There are three bottles of milk on the front porch. (Courtesy of Millie Pemberton.)

Here is the county jail before its renovation in 1935. This photograph shows the 1845 portion of the building. (Courtesy of the Tennessee State Library and Archives.)

The old jail is located on Gay Street behind the courthouse. The original portion of the jail, built in 1845, is located at the back of the current building. The front section was added in 1935. This photograph was taken in 1938. The building now houses offices for the Jefferson County Board of Education. (Courtesy of the National Archives, Atlanta.)

This was the home of George and Elsie Zirkle. Located on the banks of Douglas Lake, it was built in 1946. English Mountain is visible in the background. (Courtesy of the Tennessee State Library and Archives.)

Six

CITIZENS

It was the people that made Dandridge a wonderful place in which to grow up. Many people can recall memories of those who touched their lives. Dandridge still fosters a sense of care and service in all who call her home. Many wonderful people are gone, but many are still there. Dandridge would not be the town it has become without its wonderful citizens—both past and present.

Judge Robert Henry Hynds (1802–1856) was a member of the 21st General Assembly. He represented Jefferson, Cocke, Blount, and Sevier Counties. In addition to his role as senator, he taught school and practiced law. (Courtesy of the Jefferson County Archives.)

C. C. KRUTCH, KNOXVILLE.

Alexander Hynds is shown as a young cadet at the University of Tennessee. He was one of eleven children born to Judge Robert Hynds and Mary Jane Moore. The other children born to the Hynds were William Moore, Sarah Cassandra, George Henry, Joseph Hamilton, Sam Houston, Margaret Jane, Robert Henry Jr., David Jones, John Moore, and Ben Hynds. (Courtesy of Nancy Olden.)

Leonard and Qumille Patterson are shown in a buggy at the end of Gay Street. To the left is the Gass building, and the building next to it now houses the local barbershop. At the top of the hill is the Female Academy. Note the mud splatter on the wheels and body of the buggy and the wooden sidewalks. (Courtesy of Jean Gass.)

This photograph is of John Ellis Bettis with his mail buggy and horse. He was a rural route mail carrier in the early 20th century in Dandridge. Also pictured is his wife, Emma. The building in the background is Hopewell Presbyterian Church. (Courtesy of the Dandridge Public Library.)

This fashionable group poses in front of Shepard's Inn on Main Street. The car is a 1912 Crow-Elkhart Motor Car, produced by the M. Crow Car Company in Elkhart, Indiana. Notice the right hand drive. Most cars made in the United States before 1914 were right hand drive. The Hickman Tavern coach house is seen in the background. The brick building behind them was originally the coach house for the Hickman Tavern in the early 19th century. At the time this photograph was taken, it was the office of Dr. Joel W. Cowan. (Courtesy of the Dandridge Public Library.)

Four men pose with an Overland automobile on an unidentified street in Dandridge. Gass and Owens were agents for Overland and Ford automobiles. Their advertisement ran in local papers in 1915. (Courtesy of the Dandridge Public Library.)

Lucille and Raymond Gass were the children of James and Hattie Gass. This photograph was taken in 1910. (Courtesy of the Dandridge Public Library.)

John Talley poses with his Winchester rifle and game. His shoes were handmade. John was born into slavery in the 1830s. He died in 1935. This photograph was probably taken in the early 1900s. (Courtesy of the Dandridge Public Library.)

Pet Swann is shown at her switchboard around 1914. This was taken just one year after she started her position. At that time, there were approximately 90 phone numbers in Dandridge. She was the switchboard operator for 34 years. (Courtesy of the Tennessee State Library and Archives.)

Walter "Proc" Tinsley served in World War I. He is wearing the army medical caduceus on his collar. (Courtesy of John Shelton.)

This photograph is of Chester Rainwater Sr. in his car at the corner of Gay and Main Streets. (Courtesy of the Jefferson County Archives.)

Tine Meadows poses beside a 1919 Ford Model T. His brother Ernest is behind the wheel. Their sister Flossie is in the backseat. They are posing on the old bridge over the French Broad River. The license plate reads 1922. (Courtesy of the Dandridge Public Library.)

Will Shuler is shown on his property with his goats. Highway 25/70 eventually ran through his farm. This area of the road became known as Shuler Hill. (Courtesy of the Dandridge Public Library.)

James A. Lethco and W. Hill stand in front of Hill's Mill with one of the first trucks in Jefferson County. (Courtesy of the Tennessee State Library and Archives.)

This Sunday school class is returning from a picnic in two horse-drawn wagons in 1895. The wagons are stopped in front of the courthouse. (Courtesy of the Tennessee State Library and Archives.)

As a young boy in 1916, Conrad French sits on the mounting block in front of Shepard's Inn on Main Street. (Courtesy of the Tennessee State Library and Archives.)

Nancy Bradford was the last former slave in the area. She was born January 4, 1851 and was brought to Dandridge as a young child from Alabama. Nancy was a nurse to the Bradford family after the Civil War. (Courtesy of the Tennessee State Library and Archives.)

David Swann stands on the Dandridge Bridge, which lies over the frozen French Broad River in December 1924. (Courtesy of the Tennessee State Library and Archives.)

Dr. James D. Hoskins was the 14th president of the University of Tennessee. He was raised in Dandridge and enrolled in the university in 1896. He was president from 1934 to 1946. (Courtesy of Frank H. McClung Museum, the University of Tennessee, Knoxville.)

Bert Vincent is a well-known East Tennessee writer who made his home in Dandridge. Beginning in 1933, he started writing his Strolling column for the *Knoxville News-Sentinel*. He continued writing it until his death, which was 36 years later. Bert is shown here at 18 years old at his graduation from Kentucky State University. He was born in Bee Springs on May 4, 1896. (Courtesy of the University Archives, Carnegie-Vincent Library of Lincoln Memorial University, Harrogate, Tennessee.)

Bert Vincent founded the Cosby Ramp Festival. He is shown here in 1956 at the festival with Tennessee governor Frank Clement. Also pictured is Ellen Hynds Vincent. She and Bert were married in 1942. (Courtesy of the University Archives, Carnegie-Vincent Library of Lincoln Memorial University, Harrogate, Tennessee.)

Bert relaxes by the famous Dandridge spring in his backyard at Hynds House. (Courtesy of the University Archives, Carnegie-Vincent Library of Lincoln Memorial University, Harrogate, Tennessee.)

Bert Vincent passed away on September 26, 1969. In June 1970, the Cleveland Browns, who owned Goldrush Junction (now Dollywood), dedicated a nature trail in his memory at the park. This photograph was made at the dedication. Ellen is seated second to the right of the memorial. (Courtesy of the University Archives, Carnegie-Vincent Library of Lincoln Memorial University, Harrogate, Tennessee.)

Ellen Vincent and Paul Goddard are shown at a Ruitan Banquet honoring Bert in 1976. Paul is shown with "bicentennial whiskers," which were popular with men during the bicentennial year. (Courtesy of the University Archives, Carnegie-Vincent Library of Lincoln Memorial University, and Harrogate, Tennessee.)

Bert had a deep connection with Lincoln Memorial University and he visited often. On May 5, 1974, Stuart L. Watson officially dedicated the library to Bert. Ellen is shown here with Stuart after the dedication. (Courtesy of the University Archives, Carnegie-Vincent Library of Lincoln Memorial University, Harrogate, Tennessee.)

The Kane Family enjoys an outing on the recently created Douglas Lake. Those pictured are, from left to right, Arthur, Stephen, Millie, and Lena. (Courtesy of Millie Pemberton.)

Arthur Kane is shown in the office of his dealership. This photograph was taken in the old Jefferson Motors Dealership building. (Courtesy of Millie Pemberton.)

Neil Bradford is pictured in the early 1930s wearing knickers and silk stockings. She is holding a banjo ukulele. This instrument was popular throughout the 1920s and 1930s. (Courtesy of the Dandridge Public Library.)

Here Neil Bradford poses with Philip Eudaily. Neil was known in town for her unique talent for designing hats. (Courtesy of the Dandridge Public Library.)

In the late 1930s, this group of children plays with balloons on Dr. Tom French's front porch. Those pictured include, from left to right, (first row) unidentified; (second row) Mary Phyllis French; (third row) Donna Thomas and Everette Gantte; (fourth row) Gene Thomas, Charles Gantte, Rhea Northern, Millie Kane, and Pat Northern.

Frank Quarles was the Jefferson County sheriff from 1934 to 1940 and U.S. Marshal from 1953 until his death in 1961. He also served as a member of the Tennessee House of Representatives from 1943 to 1945 and state senator from 1953 to 1955. (Courtesy of Carolyn Ellis.)

Margaret Hicks and her daughter are standing in the yard of Margaret's home. Douglas Lake and the Zirkle home can be seen in the background. (Courtesy of Susanne Cate.)

Samuel Benjamin Hicks poses with his grandson Marty Joe Cate in 1962. (Courtesy of Susanne Cate.)

While on vacation, Merle "Zoom" Gass poses with sons Jim and Dan. Zoom's family owned and operated Gass dry goods. He was a pharmacist in Dandridge for many years and owned Gass Pharmacy. (Courtesy of Jean Gass.)

The Dandridge Fire Department is shown in the mid-1950s. Second from left is Frank Hodge. The man on the far right is Roy "Toad" Farrar. (Courtesy of Jack Farrar.)

Here is the Dandridge Fire Department in 1955. The station was located at the corner of Country Lane and Middle Alley. To the right is the Messer Shoe Shop. Jimmy Messer repaired shoes for many years in Dandridge. (Courtesy of Jack Farrar.)

This photograph shows Roy "Toad" Farrar and his youngest son, Jack, around 1957. Jack grew up to carry on the family business in Dandridge. (Courtesy of Jack Farrar.)

Here Jack Farrar poses on a bench in front of Farrar Funeral Home. (Courtesy of Jack Farrar.)

Rick Farrar walks along the sidewalk in front of the funeral home in the early 1950s. To the right is the funeral home sign. Just behind it is the Sullenberger home. The banner on the left is pointing to the First Baptist Church. (Courtesy of Jack Farrar.)

Four fishermen show off their huge catch in April 1951 at Swann's Dock on Douglas Lake. The sign on the left announces the Fishing Rodeo from April 1 through October 1, 1951. The sign on the left gives the current rates for boat rentals, motors, bait, and slips. (Courtesy of the Tennessee State Library and Archives.)

From left to right, George Hoyle Jr., Vic Arming, Guy Yoe, and Fred Astley, all of Knoxville, Tennessee, show off their Douglas Lake catch at Dandridge Landing in the early 1950s. (Courtesy of the Tennessee State Library and Archives.)

Roy "Toad" Farrar was one of the founding members of the Jefferson County Rescue Squad in 1963. (Courtesy of Jack Farrar.)

From left to right, Hope Kren, Julie Pemberton, Susan Chambers, Jim Gass, and Burney Jarvis pause for a photograph in 1964. (Courtesy of Jean Gass.)

Jim Gass (left) and Burney Jarvis play "cowboys and Indians" in their neighborhood in the mid-1960s. (Courtesy of Jean Gass.)

Seven

THE TVA

The Tennessee Valley Authority literally changed the landscape of Dandridge. In 1941, Franklin D. Roosevelt approved funding for a dam on the French Broad River. Construction was hastened by the bombing of Pearl Harbor in December 1941. The floodgates were closed in February 1943. The Douglas Dam project displaced hundreds of families and took tens of thousands of acres of land. Rich fertile farmland was forever covered with the waters of the French Broad River. If it had not been for the diligence of the citizens who appealed to Washington for a dike, Dandridge would have also been submerged below the lake.

This scene on French Broad River is looking east from Dandridge. The river bottom was once fertile farmland. (Courtesy of the Dandridge Public Library.)

The river bottom was farming land prior to the start of the Douglas Dam construction in 1942. English Mountain is in the background. This photograph was taken in 1926. (Courtesy of the Tennessee State Library and Archives.)

This photograph shows the approximate area where the ferry crossed the French Broad River in Dandridge. It was about 100 yards upriver from where the James Hoskins Bridge is now. (Courtesy of the Dandridge Public Library.)

Bridge Across French Broad River, Dandridge, Tenn.

The old bridge that crossed the French Broad River was located on the east end of where the dike is now. After construction of the new bridge, the old one was floated downriver and installed below Douglas Dam. It remained there until the early 1980s, when a new bridge was built. (Courtesy of the Dandridge Public Library.)

This shows the construction that was started on the new bridge. At the time of this photograph, the old bridge was still in use. (Courtesy of Jean Gass.)

This view is from the south side of the French Broad River looking north, toward Dandridge. In 1938, a Tennessee Valley Authority photographer took this photograph before the construction of Douglas Dam. The cupolas of the courthouse and Hopewell Presbyterian Church are visible in the distance. This is now the location of the controversial "Green Bridge" that carries Highway 92 across Douglas Lake. (Courtesy of the National Archives, Atlanta.)

Construction progresses on the new bridge over the French Broad River. The land on the south side of the river would soon be under water when the floodgates of Douglas Dam were closed for the first time. (Courtesy of Jean Gass.)

Bridge Over Douglas Lake - Dandridge, Tenn.

Here is a postcard view that is looking toward town, across the newly formed Douglas Lake. Dandridge can be seen in the distance. (Courtesy of Anne Goddard Jones.)

This is another view of the new bridge over Douglas Lake. The bridge looks much as it does today. (Courtesy of Anne Goddard Jones.)

This photograph was taken around 1942. Looking east toward Dandridge, one can see the Bethel Presbyterian Church on the left, and the courthouse cupola can be seen in the middle. The Tennessee Valley Authority built the drainage culvert. (Courtesy of the Dandridge Public Library.)

This is a view from the hill above Dandridge. This photograph was taken right after the floodgates were closed, which meant the lake was beginning to fill. (Courtesy of the Dandridge Public Library.)

ouglas Dam - Between Dandridge and Sevierville, Tenn. W-36

In 1941, the government proposed a dam on the French Broad River. The attack on Pearl Harbor in December 1942 hastened the project. Hydroelectric power was needed to aid in national defense. Construction began on February 2, 1942. It was finished in record time on February 23, 1943. (Courtesy of the Dandridge Public Library.)

Visit us at
arcadiapublishing.com

Printed in the USA
CPSIA information can be obtained
at www.ICGtesting.com
LVHW070836220224
772419LV00020B/216